Meat Lovers

MEAT LOVERS

Rebecca Hawkes

AUCKLAND
UNIVERSITY
PRESS

First published 2022
Reprinted 2022
Auckland University Press
University of Auckland
Private Bag 92019
Auckland 1142
New Zealand
www.aucklanduniversitypress.co.nz

ISBN 978 1 86940 963 0

A catalogue record for this book is available
from the National Library of New Zealand

Book design by Duncan Munro
Cover and internal artwork by Rebecca Hawkes, 2021

This book was printed on FSC® certified paper

Printed by SCG Print, Auckland

My mother, my father, my mountains.

Contents

MEAT

LOVERS

MEAT

The Flexitarian

I am trying to go vegetarian but finding myself weak,
week to week browsing the meat aisle at a linger
close enough to chill my arms to gooseflesh. I only buy
stuff so processed it hardly makes sense to call it meat.
Saveloy, nugget, continental frankfurter;
whatever gets extruded pink beyond possible memory
of the preceding body. Between the red and yellow flags
delineating the PORK section, I fondle sheets
of pig skin through their clingfilm. Flaps of fat and dermis,
bloodless as the nude silicone on a sex doll. Sad rubber
reanimates in the oven. Whimpering fat
melts to breathless squeal. The grill huffs,
fogs my glasses like hot breath. Like kissing
someone else's lover right outside her flat in winter.
Sometimes the pig has not been properly shaved. Needle
hairs prick my lips. Sometimes draw blood. Sometimes red
ink from the slaughterhouse is printed on the sallow skin.
Lipstick; damp napkin. The worst possible outcome
is unfurling the limpid rind from its plastic tray only to find
a nipple tucked inside. I try to cut it out but no knife
in my house is sharp enough. The nipple stares
a pert pink accusation. It follows me around the room.
I score the skin, scrub it raw with salt and rapeseed oil.
The nipple winks at me. Weeps in the pan as it shrinks
to helpless hiss and spit. The crackling bubbles
perfectly crisp. Blisters where I burn my tongue on it.

Help yourself

Kicked out of Countdown for kneeling
at the pick 'n' mix to sneak sweets
from the lidded bins as my mother
deliberated on fresh produce, weighing apples
with her hand while I chased the scent of false fruit esters.
Ethyl valerate reek radiating from a cartoon nuclear-waste green
gummy apple lolly. The gelatine absorbed light so it glowed
from within. Neon clot. Synthetic peridot. The fake
was always prettier and more delicious than the real apple,
the illusion of non-perishable desire magnetising my attention
beyond nutrient-rich five-plus-a-day to the synthetic forbidden.
Rascal genesis. I used my body as a shield to conceal my fossicking,
this ecstatic drooling for something I did not understand why
it was wrong to have although I had learned already
to keep the having secret. Little goblin a glutton
for the hi-fructose phosphorescent fruits
of guilty pleasure. Though how could this be theft?
The sign above the bins barked HELP YOURSELF.
But the entwined fairy mushrooms and rainbow snakes,
congealing in their own nectar, shedding crystal citric acid
and desiccated coconut shreds, all tasted the same
and made me ill. No matter how many I ate I never felt full.

Sighting

not using our inside voices
barefoot & hefting

matching backpacks
down the school bus steps

to the intersection at the edge of our farm
grass a crinkly beige & sky split ozone-blue

forgotten apple smushed under my lunchbox
leaks a dribble of sickly liquid

body temperature rivulet
down the back of my shorts

feet stickening with the squelch of tar
bubbled on the main road

inland scenic route chip seal
that gets molten every twenty-degree day

then ripped up in chunks by passing milk tankers
gouging out the infrastructure of each summer

to winter us later in potholes
that frost over as stomped ice mornings

crack & splash in our good school shoes
until the bus comes

but for now it's freckling season
sun-drenched & primal we pick

hot black bitumen off our calluses
& use it to glue dry pine needles together

into combs & swords & witch amulets
knees scabbed in the dirt we fuss & bicker

having already forgotten the slaughterhouse trip
permission slips we were shipped home with

then a brackish whiff
something feral

musks its way through the pine plantation
to slink over the state highway

brittle talismans crush in our hands
did you see it

that whiskered blackness that solid shadow
sleek haunch and broad paw

smaller than a cow
larger than a labrador

only a breathless haze where it went
heat rippling off the highway in the distance

a vacant mirage pooled between
the yellow pasture & the ordinary sky

the seeping reek
from the sack of lamb tails slumped at the side of the road

Pony club summer camp

the pony club wash up against the rocks
while you watch from the riverbank
the socks & jodhpurs stuffed into their helmets

&

the pony club offer you electrolyte drink
so much more blue than swimming pool
you expect to half die of it quenching
sharp in your throat like an eyeful of chlorine

&

the pony club argue over whether any of their true loves
could be stronger than the bond between a girl & her horse
a phenomenon so universally potent it is taken for granted
as a unit of measurement

&

the pony club braid everything with their hot freckled hands
& after weaving plaits in hay & manes & dressage ribbons
they sit in a circle and braid your hair together with their hair
& thus you become one amalgamated ponytail & so the pony club
is a sunburnt rat king

&

the pony club weep their way through the season
mucking in through gusty pollen & horsehair moult
all red-eyed unrepentant antihistamine-addled & still yelling
at you newly unsaddled to get up and quit bawling

&

the pony club have you scrubbing for hours
polishing chewed grass paste from bridle bits but they
refuse to pick the musky caked cereal out of their braces

&

the pony club dangle above your bunk on long reins hitched to the celestial
rings of Saturn & they rotate slowly with your every exhale
as though you could still move them even if
you can't quite reach from here

The Protagonists

You may ask how we knew we were werewolves,
yet like many young girls we were already familiar
with the linger of blood between our teeth, and tufts
of misplaced fur – for instance I used to get teased

for flossing with my own hair. We couldn't transform
at her house, but out on my parents' farm we practised our howls
from the tallest pine stump. The dogs looked on
bemused but unconvinced. We met in the sports field treeline

at morning tea, collecting spiny nodes of cypress
and calling them dragon eggs. We sat on our clutches
through class and reported back at lunch. I swore
I'd seen one hatch, a tiny dragonet prising open woody scales

and spreading wet wings to dry on my desk. She
immediately met this with her own five hatchlings,
flying up from between her legs to set aflame
the blobby self-portraits her class had painted earlier

and pinned by the whiteboard. She said the fire smelled sharp
like sap and I said well why didn't the smoke alarms go off.
She went quiet. I felt mean. We were meant to be
the protectors of the realm. We had sacred duties

only our werewolf powers could fulfil. Although over time
we began to question some things. There weren't even wolves
where we grew up. We needed to evolve like our favourite cartoon
monsters. So she was a weregryphon, I a werefox,

until I looked up fox-person art on the family computer
and found altogether too young that anthropomorphic foxes
had a reputation rendered in specific and instructive detail
by certain dedicated online art forums. So, for a time

I stuck to werehyena, bold and confusing, a butch choice
toying with a lineage neither canine nor feline. By then
my friend and I met every day at school to whisper the secret
wars we fought all night in our true shapes,

except when she was hanging out with her other friends
and I would climb as high as I could in the cypresses
and read until a ringing bell or teacher coaxed me down.
I spent this time considering other bodies,

still longing to writhe off my own skin and slink outdoors
at midnight as something much sleeker.
Something with so much power and grace all forces of evil
would fall before me. It so happened I had more

and more lunchtimes to myself. I worked through the animal
encyclopaedia in the library. It was there
the snow leopard came to me. That very night
I padded silent through sugared hoarfrost

in the world's most opulent fur. I savoured my own endangeredness
all weekend, eager to report my findings,
my perfect body. I located my co-conspirator sitting
with those other girls eating sandwiches under the big oak.

Don't be a stupid kid, she said to me, turning to face them.
There's no such thing as a weresnowleopard.
But there is, I insisted, nearly not-crying.
And I've got wings. There was blood in my face as I fled

and I knew all anyone could see was regular girl blood
pumping through a regular girl body even while
the other body inside mine sped up, footsteps
becoming four paws on the wet turf, faster

and faster until
   we slashed our tail out,
      spread our wings
         and were lifted.

Flesh tones

I. Her world is made on the music of meat. Heifers lowing her to sleep, smudged chalk on their haunches, mounting each other in muddy twilight. Bulls yodelling challenges. Disembodied steaks frying on the barbecue, the stovetop, the pan on the fireplace when a fresh dump of snow has taken out the power lines for another week. Emptying drips of peeled possums strung up in the neighbour's shed where she waits for the school bus when it rains. The lambs in chorus now: split from their mothers in the pens, then belly-up in the roller chute – a tower-of-terror ride for them, successive brutalities bundled for pragmatism – first, magenta vitamin injections from the thick shared needle popped through the loose skin at the back of their necks, then the clipper punching fuzzy triangles out of ears for ownership, then – for some – a fondling to apply castrating rubber rings. All this to an orderly beat of bleat-shunt-roll-pop-squirt-snip-snap-shove. Then the prolonged hiss of the tailing, a brief interminable ordeal of huge hot scissors, followed by a spritz of blowfly repellent and iodine.

II. The lambs hop back into the flock to greet their mothers. They are the future of meat. Kicking up hind hooves and waggling their stumps as if in joy once they're released – as though they've forgotten that they were only just in ultimate pain, so much they couldn't even bleat, just hyperventilate while burning bone squealed and zipped against scorching iron. Today the girl is in charge of spraying their docked arses as the lambs frolic away from their manhandlers. Their gummy open mouths are bubblegum pink.

III. When the men aren't looking she lets one suckle on her little finger. Blood tingles through her hand to swell the fingertip. She can almost believe that if the lamb sucks hard enough the cap of her nail will release and let down milk.

IV. There is trouble between the shepherds. She keeps out of their way. Confused by the jokes about eating each other's wives, she tunes out and crouches to count the tails in their stumped mounds. They are wet with a mingled glister of piss, orange disinfectant and mud souped up by all the spray. While the men pen up more lambs in the drafting race, she sorts the tails into four-and-a-bit shit-smeared batches of fifty, then puts them all into an empty fertiliser sack. Where it is still clean, the glossy white wool on the tails is as neatly curled as the dried instant noodles which are her favourite food.

V. Even the rocks where she lives look like meat, she thinks, hands in the dirt and the bloodless tails. The stone is raw-bacon pink, marbled with tallow cream and threads of iron vein. Rust traces form scarlet capillaries that bring alive the rhyolite. The volcano's slow-cooling quartz crystals pock the stone in glossy yellow pits like the open pores on her nose. It makes sense that the land and the bodies are made of the same meat because the animal bodies come from the land and they dissolve back into the dirt if you let them. Look: a sheep carcass melts home to its paddock.

VI. She went inside the earth's deep stomach once herself. Fell into the hole where the collateral carcasses are dumped. A pit carved into layers of different coloured dirt and stone, where the scrabbling claw of the digger burrowed beneath the land's new pelt of grass. Standing on the neat rectangular lip of the pasture's laceration, she slipped – landed her gumboots ankle deep in a bursting purple corpse. Round as a river rock and nearly as bald over its bloat, the ram was busy becoming dirt. The rats inside the ram ran out. Grey shapes darted into the outskirts of the hole, nests in the crevices of farm waste too big to burn. Rotted fence posts, tangled electric-fence wire, sheets of corrugated iron that had rusted everything else red as well. The smell didn't hit her until the wind changed. Sweet mordant rot like a backwards vomit, taking the worst inside. She tried to breathe through only her mouth but then closed it again in case puke got out or a fly flew in. She knows that where there's naked meat there are flies. And then, the maggots.

VII. Hoisting up the fertiliser sack of wet tails, she stands by the tailing iron reheating in its holster over the gas flame. The iron is like a hair straightener with blades which must be kept scorching to cauterise the wound as they cut. If the iron is hot enough and taken at the right steady speed, the lambs do not bleed. Mostly they don't even make noise during it – eyes the warm brown of sunshine on a cello – just gazing at nothing from each side of their prey-faces. Half a bleat barely whirring at the back of a throat as the blades click together and the loosed appendage drops to the dirt. This is still more humane than letting them keep their tails and fall flystruck. Dags caked on hindquarters invite blowflies to lay eggs. She thinks about the first ewe she found with flystrike, although of course she smelled the poor thing first, before seeing the animal's whole back writhing horribly with maggots. A squirming city beneath the green-stained wool. Eaten alive. Even meat doesn't deserve that treatment.

VIII. The tails are still warm in the sack, propped against the fence. The men are speaking again. Banter over who's going to take the brittle-boned appendages home and barbecue them, although she didn't see either take any home yesterday. Standing too close to the tailing iron as it heats, she has a slow thought that her trousers are on fire. And also, shortly after, her leg. New skin blistering, pink as volcano stone. It smells more like polyester furling back on itself than burnt wool on tailing irons, but soon there's the same savoury singed-flesh stink. Not quite the same as the lambs', but she knows for sure now that she too is made of meat. She smells herself burning and before she thinks to drop to the damp grass and snuff the fire out, she gets kind of . . . hungry. Imagines herself a future consumed. This edible girl. Her fortune of maggots. On the horizon the foothills fold like heavy cloth, unstrung curtains piled against the edge of the sky, which is a hard blue vertical surface unreal as the painted plywood backdrop of a pantomime.

Perendale princess
(after Bernadette Hall)

she grows plump as a lava flow
so earthed in her luscious volcanics
the rhyolite rose-pink   like raw flesh

and boundless   as snowdrifts   or new lambs
preciously fattening   bred for fecundity
holding dear the important qualities

of loyal mothering and rot-resistant feet
she is a rounded pebble   spilling down the gully
or an unscrolled fern   clinging to the creek's burst banks

our lady of the woolshed   in gumboots and lace
part roughshod   part dainty   the perendale princess
strokes the dead hare and   releases him

to the furrowed earth   in a place she can no longer be
a child forever   ageless baby   tiny as a lamb rib   picked clean
or generous like a mountain   maternal maiden

a reclining body   of russet tussocked hummocks and hollows
cradling bellbird and silvereye   welcome earth latticed by rabbits
but she cannot go on   surrendering to the sky

her snarling heart   caught in the barbed wire
like a skein of wool   her freezing fingers
bitter with blood   and pricked by coarse horsehair

her forehead adorned or disgraced   by an icy diadem of gorse
her pockets rattling   with spent plastic
bullet casings   in red   yellow   morbid gold

After the blizzard I followed my mother

the drifts hip-high as we pushed stiff bones through the cold to plough
a path the cows could follow, single file, into the bush for shelter –

obsidian flanks vanishing among black beech trunks so
when I stared into the abyss, it gazed back with bovine eyes.

Morning had thrown back its lid like a chest freezer to reveal too much
bleak bedazzlement. Snow filled our boots until the frost felt hot.

My mother said our service to the cattle came first, although the power
was out in the house and the needs of all the rest of us formed a torrent

like badly stacked firewood tumbling towards her, heavy enough
to crush. But the cows on the mountain relied on us; our gloved thumbs

opening gates to survival. We abandoned our candles and log burner
glow to slog through the snow and haul wet straw sheaves uphill until

the cows came home. On breaching the forest, my mother, the heifers
and I stood at the dappled sanctuary's edge, steaming under the leaves,

sweat defrosting on our bodies, in an onslaught of feeling that may have
been love (if we were allowed it) or something else as pure – sour

and insistent as the smell of silage, extreme as the glare of sun on snow.
Can you ask my mother, was she seized by that brightness?

And what if she dies while we are still angry with each other?

Waif & stray

Pastoral wetnurse shaking the dented bottles to mix
cocktails of boiled water & colostrum dust
for the orphaned lambs that skip to her & latch

on any crease in her jeans leaving patches of warm
wetness at her knees until she probes rubber teats
to toothless mouths & wells up with their total simple trust.

The older lamb, cloaked in the skin of a stillborn cousin,
struts under a stiff slink of yellowing curls — yet is still spurned
for his wrong scent by the surrogate ewe in her grief

& the younger one hops happily despite her mangled eye
pecked out by inland gulls that nest in river braids & alight
on ewes' backs to eat their newborns' soft parts first.

One big black-backed villain has since been shot
& strung on the fence in wired crucifixion, a vengeance & warning
to the karoro still circling above like a terror of angels,

a cacophony of shadows on the paddock. The lamb will not live.
The girl can smell it through the antiseptic
in the crusted socket which is not quite empty, iodine stained

& pulpy, like a knot in a school desk stuffed with chewed gum.
O mutilée still lovely, bleating, batting pale eyelashes
& those foppish lacy wrinkles at her throat –

this being the power of lambs, their softness
turning everything marshmallow darling
& so our girl is bound to serve their naïve greed

with a bottle in each fist. She has to lean back
from the lambs' alarming strength. They brace their whole bodies
against the force of their own suckling – wagging useless tails.

They tug as though to rip out synthetic nipples
with their upturned mouths & then drink up the world, chugging
hazy daylight from the atmosphere, churned sunshine

lofty as cream. On this day in Aries, the tender betrayal
of the ruminants: she will keep them warm & fed,
then they will warm & one day feed her.

But for now it is as if the girl has neither
an imminent threat of breasts nor canine teeth.
It is just her & the lambs

while all things birth & butchery happen somewhere else,
because until the bottles run dry she has no hunger
& hot milk flows from the palms of her hands.

Is it cruelty

If the sheep has a broken leg?

If the girl and her townie friend come across the sheep
on their way to the river, towels over their shoulders?
If they are already marked by the gorse etching
blood dialect on their shins, and bearing all kinds
of new beginnings with the burrs latched in their
jean shorts and hook grass in their socks,
two rough and tumble kids roaming a track
only they have memorised?

If there is nobody else around to notice the sheep,
and no nearby adult to call for help?

If the sheep tries to get up when it sees them but can't?
If the sheep's eye rolls back in its head, hazel
iris nebula billowing around the flat black
pupil? If they are two shadows that blot out
the sun reflected in said wet eye?

If the farm girl kneels down, strokes the noble
ridge of its nose, its fine elfin bone structure?
If the sheep lays still, making velvety huffs
into the palm of her hand? If the sheep not raising
itself and running seems like a kind of permission?
If they truly believe it wants to be handled and helped?

If both girls consider themselves earnestly to be druids
or nondescript mystics at home with the cycle of life and death?
If both girls kneel by the sheep and lay their hands
on it to will up all their healing power?

If the sheep stays down, not struggling, not
bleating, staring up with its one skyward eye?

If they think hard about what is merciful?

If they agree on what mercy means?
If, having no knife, they select a large stone?
If the rock is a sandstone, a river stone, rounded,
a tumbled greywacke boulder?

If it takes both of the girls to lift the stone?

If they are two shadows that blot out the sun,
holding a round black shadow that grows larger
in the sheep's eye?

If the stone hits the skull with a sick quiet thud
that is barely a crack?

If the stone rolls a little way and they have to fetch
it from the undergrowth?

If the stone hits the skull with a sick quiet thud
that is barely a crack? If the sheep makes no noise,
just stares straight up, blinking its eye? If the
stone hits the skull with a sick quiet thud that is barely
a crack? If a thin stream of blood
crawls brightly from one nostril?

If the stone hits the skull with a sick quiet thud
that is barely a crack? If they had expected it to be
quicker than this? If the stone hits the skull
with a sick quiet thud that is barely a crack?

If they had expected it take one cinematic blow,
maybe two, but now they don't know what to do,
and they are not crying exactly though their noses
are running clear snot, but they had already agreed
on what mercy meant?

If, after all this exertion, the bone in the sheep's brow
is crushed but not caved in?

If they have lifted the stone and lifted the stone
and dropped and dropped it and it no longer
feels at all like mercy?

If the sheep tries to get up but can't?

Can they walk away from it?

Can they still go swimming?

The Conservationist

I.
the farmer's daughter unbuttons
faded red overalls
rolls the sleeves around her waist
tanning topless on the quad bike
her skin is tussock gold
dewy with glyphosate

high priestess of the mountain range
she holds her spray wand aloft
incantates death diluted from concentrate
drenching the nodding thistle heads

toxins slick the silvery filigree of spines
bees unlatch from crimson eyes
spin away dizzy
jewel wings dripping penetrant

II.
the farmer's daughter surveys the back blocks
grazed stubble infested with dread rosettes
the thistles' soft explosions aloft

above the low-gear motor grumble
and the spray pump's mechanical pulse
there rises a mewling from the tree stumps

III.

the farmer's daughter digs
between the crumbled roots
loam seething through holes in her garden gloves

four kittens huddle in a deadwood knot
so new their irises still glow pale indigo
the farmer's daughter catches the slowest
its claws like crystal thistle prickles
ripping through her gloves
but now she has the kitten in her hands

what then for the pest
the mere weight of quick breath

the mother cat and the other kittens blurs already
fled into the bush

this soft furred vermin
flawless awful
psychopath in waiting
but not yet
for now it is barely the frantic whirr
of an unhinged heartbeat clutched in a palm
kneading its captor for comfort

what can she do
in these valleys
too precious with birds
to let go any fanged thing

IV.

the correct course of action
as usual
is to kill

V.

but the stream has gone dry
no puddles even for drowning
and she is too soft
to swing it on a rock

besides the farmer's daughter has lost her faith
in the hardness of stones
or softness of skulls

the kitten's pupils are slit to blindness
thin and useless as its scratches

the farmer's daughter sculpts a nest from a beanie
snarled with burrs in the bike's front toolbox
the kitten keens as she closes the lid

VI.

the farmer's daughter sloshes
like the hundred poison litres
swilling in the yellow plastic tank behind her
she is a turbid mix
of murder and croon
grim with the handlebars
thumbing the clutch

hands flexing restless
to snap necks / to caress

VII.

the farmer's daughter heads for home at hellraised speed
someone at home will know what to do
dust plumes dull her scarlet hems
clinging to the mountain
each gully and precipice
only smears in her periphery

shingle arcs in drifts
gravel clatters down the steep slip
ferns whip her shins to bruises
the spray wand falls
behind the bike

unspooling
a golden thread
a trail of wasted toxins

she turns to spot it
the kitten cries from the glovebox

VIII.

the bike goes over and over
until it stops

Noonday gorsebloom

walking the working dogs as an excuse
to spend the afternoon skinny-dipping in a slow braid of the river
meandering progeny of a fading glacier its summer-snowmelt blue
a delicious chill that stops her breath a little

the water is so clean it thrives with wriggling nymphs
stoneflies and caddis larvae and the farmer's daughter
basking in the sweat of the glacier her new limbs a half-submerged star
staring back to the sky and spitting a fountain from chapped lips

the crop-dusting plane overhead is an off-white whine in distant ozone
while the huntaways have gone off after riverbed rabbits
the willows and gorse are sizzling with cicadas
and pollinators and crisping seed heads until all the valley's music turns

muted and bluish thrummed over by her own insistent heartbeat
when she sinks to walk her hands along the riverbed
all her low submerged mounds stirring sediment
her body a sunken ship crowded with faceless ancestors

her wreckage draped with sun-slung nets of caustic light
her hair swept about like a halo of gilded didymo
until the gleaming naiad moment is ruptured by the pack of dogs
plunging in to save the mistress they see drowning

scrabbling blithe claws that raise ruddy
welts on her softened skin their clumsy strokes
cross-hatching homemade scars the numbness
of cold giving way to blazing streaks of lightning

and she cannot explain to the dogs the concept of held breath
their open mouths panting in her face
fragranced with sampled sheep shit and carrion
but the only way to get free of the mongrels' frenzy is to swim

to the shore and sit with them shivering as they
shake off their pride in salvation
so she's soaked in stinging stinking dog-water
slapping her legs from the sandflies

although the flighty vampires suckling so obscenely
are the only creatures that really belong in this scene
not the dogs or the willows or the girl
or the gorse with its raptures of yellow

that invasive stellation annexing the slopes
to wrestle black beech at the bush boundary
the smells of pollinated combat mingling by the water
sultry as marzipan and honeydew casting a heady spell

over the colonised valley the weeds like her very presence here
a legacy of other people's blood and money
though she has yet to understand this history is her own
still finding a place in her bones let alone the land

this scenery just the dappled background where she tried to leave
the body that dragged her back
and back to the world of growing things
with its own ferocious motives

still hardy like her brute inheritance that ancestral flower
named furze or whin or ulex or bloody goddamned gorse
she can be cut back and burned and still put up her tender shoots
her millions of gilded petals her seedpods cracking

shotgun blasts of life like joyous profanities
or defiant blessings like what is
this world I'm blooming into
and how might I destroy it

Quad bike farm tour

The farmer's daughter drives and I straddle behind her, our
helmets clacking together. My hands cramp white-knuckled
behind me, gripping the bike's titanium composite pelvis
rather than leaning in and holding her.
Nevertheless the bike shudders our hips
damnably close in the seat's worn incline.
My shorts ride up. Weathered cracks in the vinyl
pinch at my thighs. Her calves chafe red
in a scaly ring at the opening of her gumboots.
She has shaved her legs without moisturising.
They have the flaky silver sheen of sandblasted driftwood.
Stomping down the gear change, she slackens
her wrist on the accelerator, rolls to a lurching stop
at the gate. Waits, revving her impatience
before I realise it's my job to dismount, to unlatch the fastening.
Dust and zinc crease deep into my fumbling hands. Gorse conducts
a ragged current up the valley. Soon we are unstrung
from the powerlines that prop up the sky.
The bike purrs through the country. She's cocky,
speeding us in drifts up the metal road and rutted
tussock paddocks. She takes the crest of a hill too fast
and the bike rears up. The hind wheels threaten
to lose traction. She throws her weight
forward and tries to wrestle the hulking metal
down by its handlebars. Yells at me to jump
and I don't even say how high, I just launch myself from the bike
as though my body already knew what she wanted from me.

Trespassers will be shot
(survivors will be shot again)

tell the poachers by their beams / shafting the wild dark
/ tell the possums / by their eyeshine / the name of
which chimes / rain on the roof of the killing shed /
tapetum lucidum / isn't it just / corrugated iron singing
under static moonlight / this is before rust / seeps lurid
tendrils on the shed's concrete floor / this is before the
biggest clot of her life /

halo of moths frothed to the lamp post / solo beacon
for the dead state highway / she waits just outside the
cone of cloying light / knees clamped / clammy on the
step of the community hall / perched at the clavicle of
anywhere / locked church of the local / agnostics and
war memorialists / to gather in / its only prayer / we
were here we were here we were *here* / togetherish /
the pines are a stand of more ragged dark / the stars
are greenish in their shoals / the possums make their
routine / tortured metallic shrieks and groans / she gets
in the car when it pulls over / headlights half-dipped like
shyness /

limbs akimbo in the rhododendron grove / hand-painted
private property signage flaking off the gate / the car its
own whole animal / bloated with organs and breath /
windows limned in wet air / personal fug / pure human
chemical miasma / astringent antiperspirant / burger
wrappers like pressed flowers / cold fries fossilised
under the seats / hard spirits in mountain dew / until she
is fluorescent all the way through / her head drumming
a bruise against the switches / coming so hard the car
unlocks / rolls the window open /

unstick frigid skins / crick joints / gluey eyed / birds
tune up the pre-dawn / she treads home thrumming /
still clammy but for some / hot sore core / she has been
stoking deep / but she is needed / in the killing shed /
attending / the peeled hogget / shorn and shorn again /
beyond nude / decapitated / rigid / draining / its ribcage
slit to gape / adjustable mannequin / she imagines a
wedding dress / fashioned from corrugated iron / to
rust in / the clot plops from the sheep's opened throat /
holds itself together / stranded jellyfish in salt / it slides
out like a brave new body / freer than the one before

Sparkling bucolic

it's not real cottagecore unless you're up to the elbow in it
blindly groping down the blood-slick canal
as another contraction ripples around your knuckles
the cow is lain on her side kicking a mud angel

your hand clutching at the calf's limp hoof
head torch slipping over your brow
as you affix the chain and brace yourself
to pull and pull until an amniotic spill

when the calf's head breaches unbreathing
still you pull and bring the whole body wetly
into the cold world you drag the whole darkness
drenched newborn around so the mother can lick

caked salts and membranes from her motionless baby
as you rub her tired sides and say sorry girl I'm
sorry you're alright you're alright but somehow
the calf's ribcage has started flaring a pitiful bellows

for breath so you kneel again in the sodden grass
to feed a stalk of hay up one nostril until it sneezes
and smack its sides to keep the mucus moving
then leave them to it snuffling to learn each other

wipe the afterbirth on your thrifted silk slip
your garden strange in torchlight the red flax bowing
like a cow to her newborn the wisteria blossoms heavy as udders
loneliness collapsing on you like a waterlogged tent

Peach Teats
(calves love 'em!)

so much suckling frothy spittle and grunt
a crescent of devotees hunched at the steaming trough

barely able to breathe and drink at once
in quenched surrender to the rubber teat

their pretty eyes their pure thirsty thoughts
no useless knowledge no wondering where

their mothers are only hot sweet powdered milk
and the unique patented internal collapsing flap valve

self cleaning leak resistant flow regulating
like any perfect body or machine

Dairy queen

you're the other shedhand on the early milking shift
and you work shirtless
under your heavy rubber apron
    which I appreciate from behind –
    muscles moving under your tan
    perspiration glossy as a cold can of golden pash
unfortunately the overall effect is ruined
by your bleach-blonde dreadlocks   grinch fingers
dyed greenish by weeks of cowpat splashback

the splatter of digested turnip this morning has a smell so strong
I can hear it
as though my teeth are thirty crystal glasses and somebody
is tracing a finger along them   with skill and ease
    maybe   dear colleague   this could be you
    oh when will you   snap off your latex gloves and   oblige me

nobody would hear us
over the rhythmic chug of teat pumps with their fake baby suck
musical lactation fleshlights syncopated with radio blare
Lana Del Rey wailing
her popular summertime sadness
    I am troubled that some sadnesses are more adorable than others
    I am tired of loving people for theirs
    I resent asking to be loved in spite of mine
I've been in this mood all summer
skittish   but gentle   like a puppy
saying hello by resting my whole mouth around your hand
without biting

this is the only responsible form of tenderness:
hands limp with trust in each other's mouths
but rehearsing secret reflexes just in case

fangs clamp sharp   don't call it cynical
even though we are all secretly untrustworthy I still advocate
for getting vulnerable
          particularly when I'm 4am-shift delirious
          highly caffeinated   ripe with morning

through a slit in the corrugated iron
the moon is bright pumice   bobbing in a dark bathtub
I want to shuck off my gumboots and scrub my feet on it

I want to climb into the feed troughs while you pull the chute
so I am bathed in barley seed and spurts of molasses
          it would be the gushiest ever
          the cows could lick me clean

we milk the sick girls last
their udders so sore and swollen with mastitis
that they jog pendulously to their places by the cups
to hurry us
          their milk comes out mixed with blood
          the safe lurid pink of a strawberry milkshake
frothing into a bucket
     it looks so gross
                but so sweet

Petri dish of lab-grown meat

we have invented death without killing /
flesh without shame / noble and frigid as aliens
/ or deities / you could eat endangered species
without harming them / tell us more / explain
your insistence that this is a normal fantasy /

wall to wall ortolan / no bones or beaks / a vat
of evenly textured flesh / no more wastrel parts
/ just pure pristine meat / foetal serum from the
never-born / no more breeding stock / no more
stumbling / sighing / sensing / sickening /

no need to waste those rolling fields / potential golf greens
pugged by foot-rot hooves / no more studs /
no eugenic hunks / the bullock the rooster the
horny ram / no more traumas of annual birth /
the prolapsed ewe / the cow with conjoined twins

rotting inside her / the heifers trudging heavy with
liquid memories of absent knock-kneed babies /
giving their fullness to the metal calf that is
always thirsty / we can end these millennia
of original sin / from farm to table / in that great

manufactory of sex / it's fucked up if you think about it
/ squelching around in your gumboots /
waiting for your animals to bone / think about it
/ now think about this / exponential nuggets /
chilled in infinite vats of wobbly pink /

bottomless mincemeat / veal eternity
/ something holy about / the horn of plenty /
guilt-free / how nice to be a body without origin
/ void of complicating history / the only family
a label for the specific culture flourishing in sterility

whiteness of the utopia laboratory / and yet how
strongly do you crave the specific textures of the
entire inefficient carcass / fibrous breast or
tender thigh / surely we could stimulate this for
you in time / realdoll-customised / you could

enjoy all the pleasures of murder / without cruelty
/ you could be blushing faintly / you could feel
yourself expanding / pleasantly / to fill the silver
room / untroubled and totally satisfied / no nerves
no breath no fear no need no pain / motherless

no song or sighs no curious eyes welling with milkyway /
no sex / no sun on the skin no itch no scabs no playfulness
no leaping no glorious flex of muscle exercising
its animal purpose / every edible cell awaiting
its execution / we can solve this / ruthless ecology

/ with our miracle to end all miracles / immortality
a mere phenomenon of cellular replication /
barely trembling with the pulsing muscle memory
of the life you might have been / heartless / throbbing /
if there was a world without suffering / could you be happy in it

Dry spell

even pissing doesn't make water sounds
a frazzled sizzle in the dirt like frying bacon

sheep with nothing to do but keep grazing
nibble the dust in every direction ochre

too listless to eyeball their shepherd
as you zip yourself up to mutter *fuck this bloody place*

your family has stopped burning things
but the kids are picking through scorched rubbish remnants

paper metal glass plastics the four crucial human elements
incinerated into clots of mingled nonsense treasure

your children's fingers softened with pale ash and pricked
by incandescent filaments like witches' spindles

you miss the freedom of burning
when your lived filth disappeared like magic

and the rich black smoke plumed higher than the mountains
its close smell comforting as the half-remembered beard

you used to press your small wet face into but if tears or memories
could water the grass this bloody place would be so green

you'd have to grit your teeth and spit against its charity
while lambs ballooned from moistened earth like mushrooms

instead you evaporate among all your rusted tools and no matter
how tightly the children cling they cannot close both arms around you

Hardcore pastorals

I.

lambs explode onto the scene like popcorn
kernels such freshly detonated fluff
antigravity mammals no heart leaps higher
than the skipping lambs flocked in dozens
barely touching the ground for the joy
full fortnight in which they invent their limbs
before they settle down to their true vocation
grazing themselves into flesh factories
babies babies babies babies
the loin the chop the shank
the juicy vacuum-sealed rack
and great value barbecue meat pack
stunned slit hung bled gutted skinned

II.

damn this placid cud-chewing country
hardly redeemed by its charming panoramas
and dubious claims to purity
but if there's one thing we can agree on it's here
we appreciate the babes
admiring the taut velveteen heft
of an unmilked mammary
ohhh yes here they come
sashaying down the lane
ladies ladies ladies ladies
the ewes curvaceous yet
nimble as thunderheads
the heifers such noble slatterns
dignified curious eyelash-batters
blissed out with blessed estrus
hustling the paddock for clover
chewing cud like verdant bubblegum
and humping each other gladly
all the livelong day

III.

your baby brother points out
the window of the family 4WD
bouncing in his seat and chanting
gay cows gay cows gay cows gay cows
your father says they only put on a show
hopping up each other to get the bull's attention
but you have another word purring
a secret in your mind so fragile
if you said it aloud the air would rip like silk
lesbians lesbians lesbians lesbians
you cling to the fact that a tenth of rams
exclusively prefer other rams
even when ewes are available
this is uneconomical
but it has been studied
beyond dispute
and so are you
so are you so
are you

IV.

rabbits flaunt white arses over the paddocks
and you know you're a townie now
because murder in cold blood
is only your second thought
beyond brainless adoration
sweeties sweeties sweeties sweeties
you and your lover
have booked a cottage in the country
so you can fuck brazen
and constant as tractors
away from your too many flatmates
while roaches and moths thrash their instincts
helpless against your house of light
and throughout your sleepy morning ministrations
the rabbits perch on the edge of your veranda
bold as you like although she doesn't like
to hear you reminisce
on your buried bloodlust
so you try to tell her a cuter memory
of how the cows that sucked each other's teats
would be given a special nose ring
to discourage the behaviour
your girlfriend tilts her grin to show
the opals blazing in her septum piercing
then returns her seeking mouth to your breast

V.

in theory food is the first love anyone receives
and we hunger for comfort in sustenance accordingly
fiending for the most primal memory
of big mommy milkers everywhere
but often despite the troughs of sweetened grain
the shedhands are strangers
and there is no time to calm
each cow with careful hands and sounds
so in some jurisdictions if a cow is nervous
she may be given an injection
of oxytocin hormone
the rush of administered adoration
blushing through the bloodstream
causes her to let down milk
her body warm with amazement
what imaginings must bloom for her
as she releases herself giving over
the first astonished moments of her calf
wobbly in his new gravity or the soothing
press of her sisters at her sides or just
the barley grinding golden in her teeth
raising her tail for lovely flatulence and tingling flow
relief deflating all her tensions
to the comforting tune of the suction pump
love love love love
such a useful and necessary illusion

VI.

you like to say you are driven by love
that love takes you everywhere you need to go
because you never got your driver's licence
and your reliance on others makes you
somehow powerful
your girlfriend navigates the lanes
you gaze into the lustrous farms
naming the cows by their colours
angus hereford jersey belted galloway
friesian friesian friesian friesian
assembled by colour like assorted sweets
caramel peppermint aniseed liquorice
your mouth is watering
as you mentally concoct savoury rubs
for the beef medallions in the backseat
you are stuck behind a cattle truck
the ammonia stench of calf panic
from the slatted trailer so potent
your girlfriend punches the aircon to 'recirculate'
unwilling to even breathe the evidence

VII.

I am an astoundingly beautiful cow and I know my fate
it's a prey thing anticipating slaughter
bring out my missing sons my spoiled daughters
regardless of your romantic rural virtues
in husbandry and abundance it is nevertheless as you suspect
I know all about your mistakes and am judging you
behind my placid bimbo-gaze I calculate
the leached nitrates the cargo of conflict phosphates
the torturous farrowing crates the ever inventive
cruelties of efficiency but there are new ways
or more so old oh baby look me in the eye
when you're killing me make it personal
do not do me the disrespect of doubt
show me to the promised rotational grazing
reveal your plenteous riparian plantings
fence off your wetlands
cherish your eels and eschew intensity
because the soil still lives
and it loves on you bounteously
even in your smoky metallic cages you know it
isn't just economic
some abstract wealth-generating asset
but teacher shelter maker mother just like me
your walking temple to the womb
and all your modern systems of governance
kneel to this iconic fertility goddess
bouncing my ample natural capital up the country lane
so bitches you'd better marvel
you'd better eat drink and be merry
do not just cruise past in that decrepit subaru legacy
you feast from these paddocks already
even if you have never set foot in them
you drink the milk chlorophyll charmed in my rumen
and although you have not yet solved your problem of meat

you are something like me I think in kinship
you upright wolves you wet-eyed feeling fiends
sisters sisters sisters sisters
your tiny hearts swelling like bladders
take your place in the herd of dying things
let us jump all the fences and piss in the rivers
yes you already eat of these fields
now get down on all fours and graze

LOVERS

Undeliverance

in six eclipsed years she was all I wrote – letters
to and fro on both sides of any paper scraps
we could scrounge – always eventually the same
metronome question – all day ricocheting *are you okay*
are you okay *are you okay* – our devastations undeclared

by infinitely deflecting care with care – our love a fear
seeking laser beamed between two mirrors – we did not cherish
ourselves too well but still we wanted to offer each other
only cherished things – yet our letters were so often labelled
undeliverable – wherever we walked we looked at the ground –

low-fidelity MP3 ardour – one earbud each – worn leather
mary-janes slapping the asphalt in syncopated time –
ghostly popcorn cracking in stomachs that echoed
with guttural sounds – we sent each other any debris of hope
we found winking in the dirt – sparkles in the gutter or the bush hut

or the mall carpark – rounded quartz pebbles or blue gin glass shards
or scratched plastic rhinestones picked out between railway tracks –
there was always glitter – chosen amulets lifted from anywhere
we were not together – red jasper in church driveway chip or
scaly mica from the lakeside or fossil molluscs from the quarry –

pounamu offcuts in the grass after the A&P show – I pictured her
admiring the contrapuntal grace of the double saw final
and letting candyfloss melt to brighten her lips – how insolently
we were trying not to be organisms – young elementals
stretching our sleeves down over scabbed fists – translucent

in strong sunlight – ever reluctantly animal – unhallowed
hollows – no sanctity in our hunger – only sad bodies
craving the sumptuous mineral – I gave her something
stolen from the saltworks – a ragged crystal cluster
the rusty pink of blood in snow – we mined the world

for those small symptoms of love – our bloated envelopes
clattering with worthless treasure – the undeliverable mail
returned to us – taped at the splitting seams –
those letters too heavy with devotions –
our bellies full of paper scraps and stones

Werewolf in the girls' dormitory

the premise is simple: some are threats
and others, victims. the trick is to deflect
suspicion. to stay human
seeming. no heavy breath, no
puppy eyes. tell yourself
you don't even know
what you're capable of.
certainly you don't want anyone else to
detect the unguessed danger inside you.
press the yearning moon to the roof
of your mouth like a dry pill. bitter
painkiller. stay numbed
to accusation, or point out
anyone else among us: say this is who
flutters open amber irises after sunset, this one
reaches for other bodies in the dark
until they crumple softly, sighing. it's fun
to die briefly: a thrill of temporary
terrors. but in daylight,
nobody wants the werewolf. creep,
freak, predator, monster. so why do you want to
be found out? own up
to bloodlust. you are so close
to the girl beside you
that the hairs on your arms are growing
in front of your eyes, stretching out
towards her, lengthening into
the howl that parts the forest to pour the night in,
until the stinking dark escapes again through the windows
while all the little villagers are sleeping.

Because it was hot we stayed in the water

swimming out further / where the shadow of the mountains collapsed
slow motion on the rumpled sea / as if we were still children / tugging
the special tablecloth / from underneath the dinner party

playing secret games / between the tipsy table's uncrossed legs
our faces blurry with vanilla icing / baby teeth / unstuck
from bloody gums / lodged in a toffee apple's crystalline rind /

years later / this is just another sugar rush / parable
in which too much sweetness leads to tears / predictable losses
nauseating gaps / to nurse with our tongues all summer /

no more bitten apples / better for us to bob on the saline surface
brainlessly transcendent as the clouds / of tiny jellyfish surrendered
on the current / until we felt the chill come down / we should never

have been out so late / could hardly race our aches back to shore
where our bodies became heavy again / all goosebumps and wet towels
paralytic with closeness / we refused to get dressed / to bury bare limbs

under clothes would seal the moment closed / shatter the whipped-
meringue sky / so we stayed salt-caked / shivering / shimmering
in skins we could taste / just by laying eyes on each other

as we shuffled our feet deeper / into the sand and considered drinking
up the ocean so as not to speak / the pits we had dug for ourselves swelled
with sweet water / hotter than blood / the sun setting the sea

like jelly / raspberry / stained like your cheeks / the blush of it all
so revolting / it should have rotted our eyes in our skulls like teeth

Barbecue mirage

The national meringue sweats under its clingfilm,
pavlova leaking beads of honey like my cracked lips
where the coldsore crust has split
and weeps me salted syrup. The afternoon
pulses with perhaps. A headache
glitters in my lobes. I water it down
with a dose of sparkling sav. Pour one out for the baby
who today belongs to. Covertly bunch
my dress into my underwire and mop up
the underboob humidity. We are approaching
peak pōhutukawa. Massed stamens bristle
for a tickle of bees, flaring
their festive threads incarnadine. You
must be thirsty. You're looking at me
across the laden trestle table
as though I am a cup that never empties.
All my relatives keep saying
my life is going to change.
They nod seriously to demonstrate
their depth of sympathy. When you
thud down your spent beer bottle
the table bows like a donkey kneeling
towards me, delivering
the pav into my lap. Its gentle soak
of sweet cream creeps
up my thigh and
makes my skirt go
see-through.

Denying that it was a phase
(was a definite indicator that it was a phase)

In my black cherry lipstick and vision-occluding hairdo
my somewhat older date was wheedling me
to wear a diamante-studded leash
at a dismal fetish ball
hosted in a basement carpark.

It turned out celebrating hedonism was
quite boring actually. The display
of everyone's subversiveness
in uniform corsetry.
The trestle tables straining
under an array of handcrafted leather
at wholesale prices.

A man in white Y-fronts suspended from a cross
glowed like a novelty candle. Someone in a lab coat
dripped wax on his pale chest and prodded him
with whirring electrical implements.
He yelped and his tormentor hissed
         corpses are silent, Greg!

I could not stop laughing.
I had to abandon
the vampyre gathering.
I went for a mixed kebab.

The boyfriend was embarrassed
by my behaviour. He tried to lift me
by my throat outside Burger King
but all I could see was his face replaced by
a shouting celebrity chef, holding slices of bread
against my ears until I called myself an idiot sandwich.

I ghosted him that October. The weather warmed.
I sweated off my elbow-length fishnet gloves,
had to ditch the sweltering velvet
choker and corset as casual daywear.

It's a shame I am no longer excited
by my own badness. RIP in peace
that low-production-value manic pixie
budget goth regime, once a magnet for guys
with a low self-esteem kink, now lingering
as a custom spiked collar in my sock drawer
which I might put on until I get a hit
of self-conscious daring. Then I take it off
before leaving the house. Now when I go out
I carry my own leash.

I can be your angle or yuor devil
(know your meme)

I.

you suggested an ironic matching couple's outfit
maybe faerie queen & donkey-headed prole
the front & rump halves of a dairy cow
or for eerie pinstripe twin-suit equality
sexy bananas-in-pyjamas   patrolling golden down the stairs
the party was your idea   as all ideas are yours
& acquiescence is entirely mine

II.

I have collected hair clumps   from your brush
to rebuild you if you ever go   but in the stained
bed-linen toga   you are already half-angelic
a blessing is written on the very blades of you
which is to say   you have already holstered your torso
with the bleached feather wings I wanted to wear
& relegated me to the red foil bodysuit
it is very sweaty in here   I broil like a saveloy
ready to split from this strained crimson skin
but you are sponging my face with scarlet paint
thumb on my lower lip to steady my jaw
as you call me your very goodest evil
& you pass me the duct tape   to strap on my horns

III.

ideally I would go as a gargoyle   nothing bright
but camouflaged & crouched all night on the sagging eaves
making impeccable hentai face   mouth gaped to spill gutter water
a fountain of pure crystal puke   which you could sip from
if you wished   to hydrate   cos at the last party you got so thirsty

IV.

your pupils were huge with me in them   I wanted to stay
that way engraved   convex in your corneas
lying on some random's bed   peeling rhinestones from your cheeks
your fingers tracing the red inside out of my ears
swirling fingerprints like record grooves
a whisper   louder than music
so when you left I just lay there listening
a soft shell echoing your sounds

V.

unable to plead you to stay in the crumpled coverlet
or to let me leave with you   unsure even what it was you had
needed that evening   a touch of poppy or psilocybin
probable acid for the base brain meat
or syruped cactus hewn from a neighbour's plot
not that I was sober by any means   the room scintillating
purple and gold like an ametrine druzy
but I was already braced for the descending tonnage of dawn
while you partied for no tomorrow   life & soul etcetera
always telling me *ugh dude*   *your reality is stifling*

VI.

you are so very titania
you could elevate any tacky sequin gown
while I pose in the background
you may even plant a kiss on my equine novelty mask
but I listened in class   reading the rohypnol empress
when the husband-potion pins back her lashes to wow
at any passing ass   listen I'm not bitter
to not be chosen   listen   it's worse than that

VII.

cos it was me that found you later
strewn in someone's lap

room cloyed with cold vomit & molten
bodies   I carried you through
the terrible fairy lights   flashing in the hallway
where you mumbled *no cops no cops no*

VIII.

gathered you home   showered you
without looking   & tucked you in
jettisoned a drink bottle squeeze through clenched teeth
hand-fed you what I could find   white toast & margarine
salty petals of shaved ham   a generous spoon
of whole-egg mayonnaise   & I lay awake
on a mound of damp towels
in the blankness   between your shallow inhalations

IX.

I still believe   if I'd had to
I could have breathed life into you
despite this craven mouth
too shy to say
why do you still hang out with those people
or   *dude u know I l*ve you*
but I don't know how to help you
probably I should have started by simply saying   *nah*
not this time babe

X.

& yet today   I seriously contemplated the cow costume
with no question that you would lead   our doubled bulk
as I bent over   holding your hips   to follow blindly
the bell at your collar   ringing in the beautiful boys again
to name them more wistful things than me
peaseblossom   cobweb   moth & mustardseed
because you are the sugar eater
& the night   the night is full of nectars

I'll eat you up I love you so

during the bad dryad phase I was constantly performing violences /
unbinding rampant vines with my machete / cradling a bottle of
bleeding heart / I thought you understood this / stumbling into the
undergrowth / as a nymph made of wood / I only knew how to burn

I crawled from the thicket to live in a society / I wore a praying mantis
to the party / my primordial ornament / curtseyed like a lady / a
cultivated wildness / danger plaything / my wandering hairpin of
lemony emerald / as poised as a god and as silent / pinned to my shoulder
/ I propped myself on the balcony / with casually inebriated grace /
pretending to inhale / until a carapace grew resolute around me / my
body still an unsprung trap / my wicked razors held tight to my chest

I no longer belonged to the bulldozed grove / my childhood was no
longer a real place I could return to / my bark peeled back to sapwood
slickly waxen / the fresh skin a moonstruck spearmint / magnolia
ombre roseate on my blossoming terrors / my forearms tidy scythes
/ flexing to compel you towards my ardent mandibles / half petal half
predator / after all a nymph is just the youthful form of mantis / and I
am an orchid's deception / new hungers shimmered through my lymph
/ like treacherous auroras

now if you are the knife I am the slice / of wagyu tenderloin / in the
softcore food porn / revolving on the showroom television screens
/ burnt butter caramel slo-mo drizzling over whipped cream / or a
glamorous bloodthirsty rainforest scene / if you are a sphinx moth I am
an orchid mantis / posing in the epiphytes / people will let you be cruel
/ when you are beautiful / I am trying to look like a good green thing
for you / but deep down I'm a decadent consumer / all mindless
appetites / imitation flower greedy / doing my menace shimmy /
come hither come hither come / here / let me hold you in my arms

Lesbian vampire film theory

//
a circle of witches dancing starkers in the meadow
buzzed on ergot and fly agaric but there is no forest and no coven
it's just you and I holding hands in public

//
mentally I am already weaving my wedding dress
from cobwebs and posing in it to collect dew
under the lettuce misters in the vegetable section

//
sluttish unsubtle I am tossing assorted clefty stonefruits at you
I am rubbing my nose in a burst fig foraged from the brambles
sucking the drunken wasp out to spit it down your shirt

//
I am sweating rivers like a cocktail glass full of ice
when you have already slurped up my heady dregs
and demanded another   another   bartender please   another

//
you have spawned something so fluorescent in my braided veins
at first I thought it was wrath but it was whitebait those endangered brilliant
millions   all visible organs   and flickering hearts exposed

Poem about my heart

you have one job
which is to hold

this disturbingly large moth
battering the woven
basket of your fingers

every instinct whining to
close your fist and crush it

or open your palms
set the fluttering insect loose
free your hands for other tasks

but this is your job
the having and the holding

the moth beating scaly wings
moonstruck dust tarnishes your skin
putrid silver as you do not ask

how did this thing get in here
just maintain your grasp

on the fragile lunatic alien
that flew to your light and would not leave
until you caught it and kept it and it became yours

Mad Butcher's love song

You're the pent-up lady of the colonial station
and I am your farmhand, precarious hayseed
dangling from my lip, the ill-mannered
hooligan folding you like scone dough
over the coal range in the musterer's hut.
Because it is your preference I have not wasted time
on tenderising. You sputter and waver like a wick
wet with kerosene. Like a good keen man I mercilessly dirty
the butcher's blade at my belt. You borrow my knife
to carve lumpen lovehearts into the bunk's greasy slats.
If looks could really kill you'd mount me
as a trophy in your dining hall. Instead you take a needle
to my neckerchief, apply prissy embroidery
proclaiming *women want me* and
fish fear me. When I tickle trout
from the silty creek to sate you
on bloodless flesh, we cannot help measuring
our grievances to establish whose is bigger.
I have no real desire to wound you
but I could take you down a peg or two.
So ask me not for whom the mountain oysters toll . . .
Shepherdess, cocking your crook, you bad-bitch Bo-Peep,
I am aware that in your breeder fantasies
you would replace me with any red-faced leather-fingered
young farmer of the year – eyes glazed with toil,
his act perfunctory and absent-minded as a ram's,
testes swinging like tongueless bells
pealing strenuously for thee.
They say the old station-holders used to castrate lambs
to wethers with their teeth – isn't that your area
of interest? Hard men rousing on the muster
posing the evergreen question: to spit or swallow?
But think how tender those shepherds must have been
with their incisive surgery – the cutting kiss –
and all that bleating. Can you even imagine the care I take

when care is asked of me? Yet I only work for you
as a man alone, butch, bullish. Someone stone; stinking
of smoke, lanolin and oilskin; wielding a hoof pick
for lambs' blood crusted under bitten hangnails;
a roughshod cowpoke callused to the soul. My utility
is singularly in hardness, the fool gored up to the hilt
to prove your own honed steel to yourself.
I'm a tool. If you could bear to comprehend
my gentle nature, this would be a real affair.
Instead I pack my softness down like snow.
Still, the longer this goes on, the more my insides
go to pulp, fizzy as fermented wild apples.
Soon it will all seep out and you will have to choose
a sunset to ride into. For now, saddle up.
Once we have obliterated each other again, come out
beyond the long drop. On one knee I'll offer up
my only other secret: let me show you
how I make the moon shine.

The stars are looking down on us

and boy howdy are they judgemental
sneering in twinkles at our histories
of malpracticed lust
and crooked orbits
the dim little glows of us
in each other's screens
or beds or cars or abandoned
sports fields anywhere
we can press our skins
together till we spin out
only to collide again
persistently trying to get it
right with our temporary
hands and mouths and
other relevant nerve endings

meanwhile the stars are expert flirts
sexting through light-years
they bone entirely in morse code
and are satisfied

                              (only the occasional comet
                          burning its wants through the sky
                        betrays a celestial body's true desire
                              to be touched or die trying)

Mince & cheese

you brake too hard and blammo
I have crushed the half-bitten pie in my hands
deflated pastry relieved of its high-protein load
the flimsy plastic sheath serving no protection
from sticky mess jettisoned hot across cheeks
and dripping from my chin to form a savoury crust
that tightens and glistens across my lips
such that you have no choice but to pull over
cursing at the next picnic stop and
lick it in the way you will my wounds

The salt lamp I got you for your birthday

hooks up to your computer with a USB. It needs to be plugged in all the time. Blooming peach-pink it is a spherical lukewarm heart that does not beat but glows in the dark. It is heavy in your hand, a satisfying weight, a wee watery Mars plucked out of orbit. If you unplug the salt lamp from its arterial port not only does the little LED inside go dark but the salt lamp starts to sweat out all the moisture it has sucked up from your humid room. The salt lamp is always thirsty. It drinks and drinks. Then it weeps out its skin like an elderly boiled sweet. You lick the salt lamp and it tastes salty. Honestly I don't know what else you expected. The salt lamp says you've got to learn that everything is historical; maybe you should read some Marx. The salt in your salt lamp was mined in the Himalayas. The workers who mine the rock-salt chunks by hand for lamps like yours, are supposed to be exceptionally happy and healthy people because this kind of salt is just so very good for you. Isn't that great to know? It does some stuff with ions apparently, good stuff that regular table salt with the same chemical composure just won't do. I feel better already, don't you? But you have forgotten to plug in the salt lamp. Sitting in your dark room deep in laptop-screen light you shine blue. The salt lamp licks you.

Cute trip 2 the zoo

when we can no longer bear to observe each other's habits
we go to the zoo   admire its resolute
conservation values
in the face of   you know
            everything!!!!!!

the happy otters   fiddling   in their delightful water feature
the lions in their vast and stately boredom
the apes making do
            infants dangling at their breasts
            like heavy medals

we are watching the giraffe wrap its grey tongue
around a weeping child's arm
when you ask me for a nature poem   I'm like
            woof!!
I recite a documentary ode
to traumatic educational television

the comic whiskered walruses in slow motion
lumbering over the cliffs
their bodies falling like
                  sacks of   wet meat
            hurting!!!!!!!!!!!!!!!!   until they stop

there's no pretty lyric for it
only technically remarkable drone footage
imprinted on the eyelids

you and I do not deserve 'nature'   or 'poetry'

no tusks no flippers   my kind at least   have earned nothing
but unpayable debts   since we crawled out of the sea

what do you want from the bloody nature poem anyway

a romance   for the blind and desperate   beasts
            hunkered together
            out of desperation   not out of choice
aha   oh so now you tell me   you want me
to make the world nice!!!!   to say one nice thing!!!!!

well   even if I were a universally beloved naturalist
with a soothing colonial accent
narrating your behaviours
in sympathetic detail
you would still want someone else

a runway judge to proclaim you foxy   on a weekly basis
            'the next big thing!!!!!'
or   a distinguished warrior
to grip the back of your neck   in silent approval

the slack-jawed tiger disregards us   pacing her perimeter
into a muddy trench

apparently they're not even soft!!!   you say of the walruses
            you tuck two chopsticks   under your top lip

you bark you whistle you groan   some people stare
but most don't look at u
            they are purposefully not looking

but you are committed   flopping around
until you lie still on the ground by my feet
            where I kick you gently
            until you stand up

Pink fairy armadillo

One of your axolotls has eaten the other
and every week you clean its twenty-litre tank
of cannibal excrement. I consider your commitment
to caring for that stunted salamander.
However rancid its clownish ruff,
it will always be your baby. And I
will be what exactly? Above your bed
you have thumbtacked photographs of a stag
chewing its own sloughed velvet like wet jerky
and a pair of bumblebees at worship
in the upsetting symmetry of a passionflower.
Beneath the grubby dog-eared splendours of nature
sex churns inexorably towards us again
like a combine harvester. All I can attend to
is the cryptic grin of the axolotl
settling among its pebbled substrate
like a blob of watermelon gum
with all the sweetness chewed out of it.

When we have threshed our chaff sufficiently
you describe the other woman. You have become
indisputably feral to me, but do I disrespect you
like a pigeon or fear you like a seagull?
Those madly avian eyes, blank and greedy.
That scavenger instinct, always taking a bite out of whatever
I am eating, even if it is the very last morsel on my plate
because I have been saving it. I used to relish
your minor evils – a barb, a prick, a sting –
an acceptable level of nemesis when I still believed
selfishness was honesty. You had been the first
jerk in a chainmail jerkin at the renaissance faire
to observe that my suit of blush-pink armour
was decorative but not functional. If you punched me in the tit

the generously sculpted breastplate would puncture
my sternum, killing me instantly. Yet my love
in that moment was a ravenous animal
that would eat from any outstretched hand.

Once you told me two mammals buried in a snow cave
would not consume each other because it is better to die warm
than alone. How humiliating that I have sought
to burrow into the flesh below your chest
a pink fairy armadillo trembling for safety
the kind of paradoxically precious wild creature
that cannot even survive in captivity. Is it too much to ask
to be universally adored? Have I not been
a ruby-throated truth to you? I could be as ruinous
as an orchid mantis shimmying, or as toxic
as an almond-scented shocking-pink dragon millipede
dripping cyanide syrup. I have contemplated
chewing off your tongue and replacing it myself
like a parasitic louse in the mouth
of a roseate snapper. But it is best to shed my skin
like a magenta-scaled eyelash viper, and leave it
folded neatly on your pillow – my fangs much longer now,
your fish tank empty but for its shifting weeds,
the filter groaning and squelching out
beleaguered little kissing noises in the dark.

I know where you live
(I used to live there too)

You held me only briefly in the doorway. I couldn't smell her at all,
pressed in the depths of your purple floor-length puffer jacket,
which stank of its same old simple comforts; weed exuding

through the lumpen goose-down. It was almost tolerably
freezing inside that house. One plunger of wrung-out grounds
steamed up every window. You didn't offer me a cup.

I opened and closed kitchen cupboards, seeking any clean vessel
to load up with bitter warmth. My chosen mug was merchandise
peddling a charitable cause, the rim circled with an affirmation

turned desperate by too many ellipses: *I'm making a difference......*
I'm making a difference...... I'm making a difference...... I'm making a
difference...... Inspecting the pantry I dipped my finger in your lover's jar

of half-fermented honey. Smeared a gob across the lip. You refused any,
just continued to sip and wince at the stale coffee, raising your face
from a mug so large it fit an entire soup recipe down the side in peeling

cursive script: the procedure required an entire desecrated carcass,
bones already picked. I tried to tease – why didn't you just add milk
if you were going to be a baby? In sullen retort, you advised me to kneel

down and moo before suckling on big dairy's udder, then rambled on
about how the caffeine served a need so it wasn't necessary to pretend
it was sweet. I called bullshit. Given temptation you'd be the first to live

deliciously; so stoned then you could hardly form coherent sentences,
when it was you who'd asked me to come over in the first place.
How had I remembered your fakery fondly? My heart a stupid oyster

forming a pearl around a plastic microbead. But here I was, chilling
in your kitchen. Where could I sit? What should I do with my hands
if they weren't on you? Feathers worked their way out of your jacket

shafts first. How I wanted to pluck you. Behold, a featherless biped!
And now, another game of chicken. I attempted to be noble. Even with
your fist in my hair, agonies flaring on my scalp like birthday candles,

I asked how things were going with her. You said, it is what it is.
I felt I could keep you, like a persimmon on a sunny windowsill. Still
waiting for your heart (I know, I know) to ripen. Soft and sweet enough

for me to want to bite a hunk right out of it. Your heart did turn slippery
like persimmon jelly; brittle as pearl nacre gilding the irritant. Yet I have
seen the discarded mattress in your garden, overgrown by onion grass

and tradescantia. The stuffing is soggy, but I can sit there and write,
or hitch cicada husks by their sickle claws into the skin of my upper arm
and call to see if you'll rise from the couch; help me pluck them out.

With your one mild and precious life

I am as frenzied as this automated airport toilet
that flushes constantly while I sit on it
each oversensitive gush an excess moistness

wasteful but also flattering
the hopelessly devoted motion sensor
does not simply let it mellow

I respect that singular obsession
I am brewing a hot disdain for the meek and tepid
and for all weak bathroom hand dryers

I wish for scorching gasps to push the skin
away from the bones of my hands
wicked airblade whittle me

down to blackened talons that could sever
the straps of your carry-on baggage
claw forgettable airport literature from your grip

but I merely wipe my hands on my shirt
wrap my arms around you trying not
to touch your neck with clammy fingers

I let you go easily and you are not detained
by airport security or by my amateur telepathy
pleading without making a scene

you place your backpack in the scanner tray
I am waving and waving and you are through the gate
you are out of sight and my hands are so so dry

Leftover ode

another day / another unclaimed
tray of mince in the fridge / no lid /
not even a wispy modesty of clingfilm
to veil the waft maturing in its nameless

greyish nodes / permeating the white-walled gallery
of nutrition / the window into a household's soul
being via the refrigerator / our aspirations
of fresh green selves / irresolute / the intact head

of lettuce sloppy in its plastic sheath / wizened
carrots blackening / beetroot tempeh burger patties
no longer crimson / their meatless bleed
luxuriant annihilating fungal cerulean /

and the once burly silverbeet now limp as a newborn's neck
but the mince is still most odious
slumped at the centre of everything / numb punch
to the retch-cortex / a dull though unsubtle power

converting its neighbours to echo its essence / infusing
even the warping slice of meat lovers pizza
I saved for you / though the cooler
has curled the crust to a cardboard hangnail /

gleaming medallions of stiff pepperoni
precious as opalised fossils
in a cretaceous bedrock of cheese / but
somehow it still seems worth keeping

in case you come home
and are hungry

Grazing platter

it is unfeasible to organise my life around desire
but convenient to define it by mealtimes
     so the lavish sap that paid for my evening's amnesia
     is helping me forget you
     expensively

but oysters stick in my throat
like necking salty shots of cold snot
although I just about enjoy the semi-coarse pâté
until considering cat food wet from the can
     the cursed mouthfeels
     of aspirational luxury

my faceless benefactor asks what I am looking for
but I just want what all women want
     if not vengeance in cold blood
     then at minimum
     a bargain

strange to think I could once strip
the skin from a possum in one fluid rip
or that I'd ever been wooed
to tunes of throbbing gristle
     as the piercing tongues of the fine-dining violins
     wheedle through my sensitive organs

I am preparing for the impact
where my prosecco glass meets
the flashy granite countertop
     I will slit necks with the shards
     and drink and drink and drink my fill

Any crystal can purify you
(if you are sufficiently committed to stabbing
yourself through the heart with it)

selenite splintering my lungs fibre-optic
or a wand of polished labradorite that refracts
my fractured ribcage into a dozen shades

of feldspar glint oh dear I had forgot that slick jade egg
charged in distilled windowsill moonlight for this ritual
I the jewel-sucker swilling mouthfuls of tropical smoke

encrusting myself with a semi-precious geode
in the hopes that beauty could ever heal anything
these jagged stones with their accidental loveliness

grown in earth for no one's eyes   yet fetishised
into the sickness of the supply chain   the miner's sons
hunched underground scraping out tourmalines by hand

the middleman at the port town exchanging
a cup of rice for a kilogram of rose quartz
sold by a peroxide wiccan at the gypsy fair

with a promise that it would bring me love
and yet my heat-treated citrine loses its vibrance
in the glittish glare of direct sunshine

and the oily rainbow aura on the spirit cluster flakes off
as the titanium enhancement fades   while I   still addicted
to new knowledge   in my liquid crystal display   can finally scry fate

from this obsidian mirror   scrolling the oracle screen
for every treasure on my mantelpiece
a child's hands digging

Nepenthes terrarium

I have named the pitcher plants
Lil' Jugs, Big Naturals, and Juicy Caboosey.
I like to see them dangling, those
carnal cups both pendulous and gaping,
sun-beamed so the veins bulge in their throats.
The pitchers drool when they are happy,
oozing sugar syrup from their pores
to which I say: girl, same. I am no longer at war
with the ants that rally their colony's regiments
up my bookshelf directly into the puckers
of Juicy Caboosey's rigid lips. She reddens,
ridged with her pleasures, her glut betrayed
by the dim shadows of still-twitching bodies
collected in the morgue sac. Macabre – but houseplants
will make this neglected investment property a home. I keep
my apartment humid, claustrophobic air obliterating all
distinction between inward and outward breath. My love language
is acts of service. I water the sphagnum moss at the roots
and catch the plants more complex nourishment. I learn
to move without stirring the unventilated atmosphere
to catch flies against the windows, pressing pale gold guts
into mildew-gilded rivulets of condensation. As the pitchers grow
engorged with vitamins, I seek out larger prey. Lure
mice from their nests between the studs, then trap the merry rats
that flit in the bowels of the communal rubbish skip.
The body corporate holds a special general meeting
to account for the disappearances of residents' cats. I perch
beside the complimentary refreshments, conditioned air
rasping on my skin, my absent landlord's vote an affirmation
to install cameras at the building's entrances. No matter, I only need
to keep the pitchers fed until his next inspection, when he will learn
headfirst how to add value at last, if only as fertiliser. If the pitchers
are not yet large enough, I have looked up where to saw the joints.

Add penetrant to preferred broadleaf herbicide
(& devastate the wildflowers)

//

        an overabundance of lupins scours the Mackenzie Country
scorched pestilent amid shallow rabbit digs & wildling pines
glacial sediment pigmenting lakes   blue as the cyanide-
spiked bliss balls we cull wallabies with
Ferafeed 217: Peanut Butter Classic
           local farmers are obligated to eliminate the lupins although a
few plant them on purpose   contentiously
providing forage-fodder for merino sheep in the high country
they're pretty   these weeds
deep rooted & pernicious   shedding
protein-rich seeds & a kind of shade that only other unwanteds
can live beneath

//

        in a carpark on the shore of Lake Tekapo
        the rabbit gets shot over & over again
        yet will not die

a squad of amateur photographers line up
as the rabbit hustles into the lupin thicket

    where I crouch low unspotted by the throng
    their lanyards & itineraries
        to snap up unpopulated scenery
        in a picture I will not send you
snow-capped peaks etcetera   & of course
the noxious pastel tapestry
        a cheap pixelated sunset
        an aestheticised bruise

plus a rabbit that poses for me like warm taxidermy
      half the sun cupped in its silky earlobe
      blood vessels ignited petal-pink

I expect the photo could win an award at the A&P show
if they hadn't banned pictures of the stupid lupins
                        the lazy ease
                                of such inconsiderate loveliness

the tour bus moves on   the rabbit and I remain

//

                        all humanity's accomplishments
                        are due to a six-inch layer of topsoil
                        & the fact that it rains

//
        where it won't rain we irrigate
                until the green believes us
crop circles patrolled by centre pivots
                unparching the lucerne   the clover   *hieracium*
        this false precipitation this sun shower of effluent
rainbows glinting from the fine spray of shit

//
so much depends on
            whether the sheep are hungry enough
                        to tolerate the taste of toxic alkaloids

as the lupins bloom out the summer in their splendid blushing colonies
        both the planters of lupins & their weedkiller neighbours insist
        that nature should take its course

but they can't agree on what nature means:
conserving shrivelled unpalatable tussock or letting slip
the lupine war on the landscape   floral battalions

whose thorns do you prefer
sweet briar-rosehip or matagouri

//
        the lupins lend their purpleness to prose & I
        am ill-equipped to be alone
with this sentimental glut   a too-easy picturesque
florid & fecund & phallic   all guzzle & loll
        choking the riverbed with sex
ovaries & stamens   orbicular pods   naked waxen stems
        little pink hoods yielding   like inside-out skin
        fallow on bedlinens which still reek   of cross-pollination

clearly   I haven't buried the hatchet   I am still swinging it
in my splintered fist   I am building a tiny house with it
in the Mackenzie Country
because I cannot live inside you

//
meanwhile the lupins   wring out their bright disaster of seeds
in the riverbed   & propagate downstream

Depth imperative

You have been communing with the eels all morning.
Dangling last night's gnawed pork bones over the creek
while the slimy puppies knot over themselves
in gambolling brawny glutinous undulations,
the river's working muscles making kissy faces

to beg at the surface for flesh. You are adopting
an attitude of manic gratitude, walking barefoot
to the swamp to flaunt your scraps. Waxing on
about how the sequin-eyed species flexes through the torrent
to breed far out at sea, maybe swimming so deep

their bodies disintegrate, and spawning glassy larvae, the
elvers silvering homeward up the last clean catchments
to lurk in the shade of trailing ferns. The more you know of the world,
you say, the more you are compelled to devotion. Once you are done
congratulating yourself, you retreat to your studio. By night

it fills with moths and giggling lizards. By day the rooms drone
with blowflies. You press your finger to the pesticide aerosol
until your print whitens on the trigger. You hold your breath
while the insects gyrate deadly burnouts into silence. A song comes on.
You don't know where you've heard it, but you know the lyrics by heart.

Thanks

To all the friends and fellow artists who glow up the world with your devastating brilliance. This wouldn't be a book without your insights, tight fives and ego boosts. Thank you hype beasts, show ponies, leading lights and coven mates: Tor, Razz, Nikki-Lee, Sinead, Claudia, Jordan, Essa, Erik, Freya, Chris, Sam, Tayi, Joy, Jackson, Caro, Ruby, Rose, Ash, Stacey, Ella, Caoimhe, Pip and you, if you've ever dutifully listened to these poems or thrashed an evening of karaoke into the morning with me. It's an honour to read and write with you, and to share the mic at TK BBQ.

To Sam, Louise, Duncan, Sophia and the AUP team for your care and humour through perpetually unprecedented times.

To Verb, *Starling*, NZ Pacific Studios, the Robert Lord Cottage, NZ Young Writers' Festival and *Newsroom* – thanks for providing opportunities to work on this collection. Thanks especially to Gaye and Michael for your hospitality and the merriment of eels in your backyard where I wrote so many of the poems that became *Meat Lovers*.

To the publishers that first offered homes to poems from this collection – *Starling, Mayhem, Cordite, Turbine | Kapohau, NZ Poetry Shelf, Landfall, Sport, Newsroom, Out Here: An Anthology of Takatāpui and LGBTQIA+ Writers from Aotearoa, Aotearotica, Salt Hill, Scum, Bracken, Nine Magazines* and *Stasis*. Special thanks to Louise (again) and Francis for the crucial platform you've built for young writers in *Starling*, and to Hannah, Magnolia and Morgan for our beloved *Sweet Mammalian*.

To my parents Jeanette and Murray for raising me in the most beautiful elemental corner of the world, and teaching me to attend to the land with a scientist's sense of wonder. To my brother Campbell, fellow mountain roamer, river swimmer and snow chaser, for trudging up Mount Alford with me even when it was raining. To Te Maka Kaha and the north branch of the Hakatere river. To Digby, Blackberry and Charcoal, noblest of cats. To the thousandfold other animals I have fed and/or eaten.

To Scott – best friend and lover of mine – where would I be without your constancy? Hangrier, and much less happy. Thanks for being the reason to write that poem about my lucky, blundering little heart.

Author photo: Ebony Lamb

Rebecca Hawkes grew up on a sheep and beef farm near Methven and now maintains a tenuous work/work balance in Wellington city.

With poems widely published in Aotearoa journals, Rebecca's debut chapbook 'Softcore coldsores' was published in *AUP New Poets 5* for the reignition of the series in 2019. *Meat Lovers* is her first full-length collection.

Rebecca is an editor for literary journal *Sweet Mammalian* and the climate change poetry anthology *No Other Place to Stand* (Auckland University Press, forthcoming). She is a founding member of popstar poets' performance posse Show Ponies and haphazard coordinator of the Pegasus Books poetry reading series.

When not writing, painting or gainfully employed, she can be observed painstakingly catching insects to feed her spoilt pitcher plants.